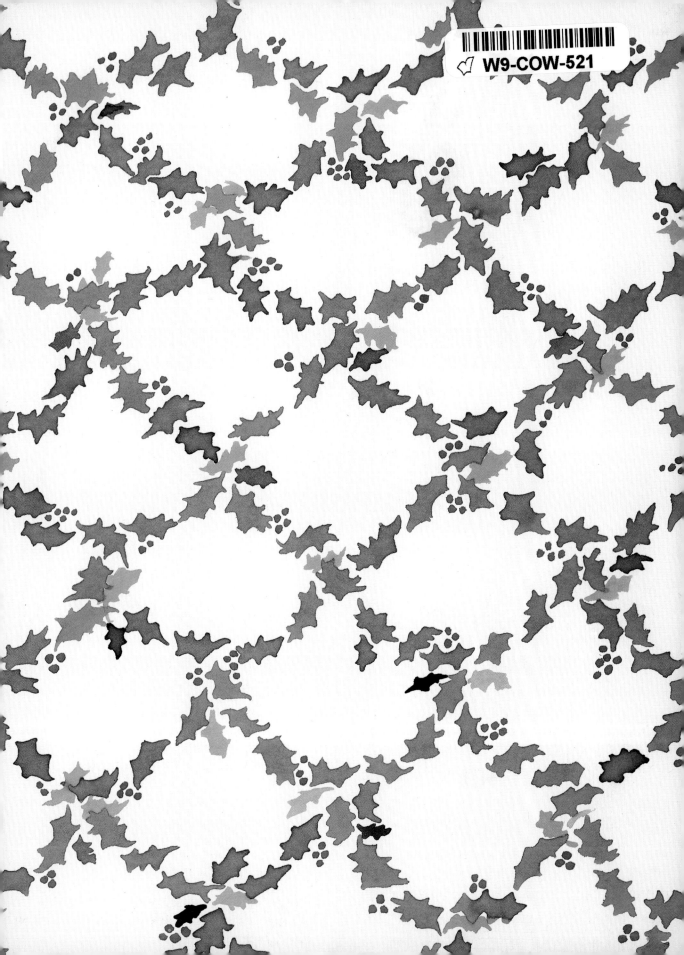

Our Christmas

This book is for
the _____ Family—
to remember in years to come the warm
and happy Christmas
we spent together in 19 ___.

Our Christmas

Illustrated by
Hans Wilhelm

Published by Grolier Enterprises Inc.
Danbury, Connecticut

Grolier Enterprises Inc.
Robert B. Clarke, Publisher

ISBN: 0-7172-8179-5

Printed in the United States of America

TABLE OF CONTENTS

A CHRISTMAS ALPHABET

Here is a Christmas celebration, spelled out from A to Z,
a list of words that sketches in the season.
But don't look for *Xmas* or *holiday sales*—they're not
here for a reason.
This is a good old-fashioned ABCD-iary,
speaking of peace and joy and love,
wishing every Christmas heart be merry.

*A is for Angel,
bringing peace and love
to Christmastime.*

*B is for Bethlehem,
tiny village where
the wonder began.*

*C is for Carols,
Christmas songs
of joy and praise.*

*D is for Doll,
lovable new playmate,
hoping to be hugged.*

*E is for Eve,
the night before Christmas,
when Santa comes our way.*

*F is for Fruitcake,
rich with the
holiday's bounty.*

*G is for Goose,
cooked to a turn
for our family table.*

*H is for Holly,
green and berried,
shining Christmas branches.*

*I is for Icicle,
winter's gift for
our snowman's nose.*

*J is for joy,
born of the
Christmas spirit.*

*K is for Kings,
who came to see
and stayed to adore.*

*L is for Log,
spreading warmth and cheer
on our Christmas scene.*

*M is for Mistletoe,
granting good wishes
for our holiday kisses.*

*N is for Noel,
another name for our
Christmas tradition.*

*O is for Ornaments,
to hang on our tree, bright
and silver and heavenly.*

*P is for Presents,
lovingly wrapped,
hiding sweet surprises.*

*Q is for Quilt,
on which a cat can nap and
dream of Christmas catnip.*

*R is for Reindeer,
Santa's kind helpers,
who make the sleigh go.*

*S is for Santa,
jolly old gent, heeding
the letters we've sent.*

*T is for Toys
under the tree, each one
saying, "Come play with me."*

*U is for Up,
up in the heavens, where
the Christmas star shimmers.*

*V is for Visitors,
welcome are they to
our Christmas celebration.*

*W is for Wreath,
happy sign of
a happy season.*

*X is for Xylophone;
on it we'll play the
Christmas songs we treasure.*

*Y is for Yule.
Three cheers for the feast,
and gifts for even the least.*

*Z is for Z-Z-Z-Z,
a sleeping child
dreaming Christmas dreams.*

Dear Santa

At this very moment, Santa and his helpers are busily at work making Christmas presents for all the girls and boys in the world. From his workshop somewhere near the North Pole, Santa sends children this urgent message: "Please write and tell me what you want for Christmas, so I can bring it to you." You can write your letter to Santa in this book or on a separate sheet of paper. But don't forget to write!

_____

_____

_____

_____

_____

_____

_____

_____

_____

_____

_____

_____

_____

_____

_____

_____

_____

_____

_____

_____

_____

_____

CHRISTMAS POEMS

Sing hey! Sing hey!
For Christmas Day;
Twine mistletoe and holly,
For friendship flows
In winter snows,
And so let's all be jolly.

Traditional English

Christmas is coming. The geese are getting fat.
Please to put a penny in an old man's hat.
If you haven't got a penny, a ha'penny will do,
If you haven't got a ha'penny, God bless you.

Traditional English

Long, Long Ago

Winds through the olive trees
  Softly did blow,
Round little Bethlehem
  Long, long ago.

Sheep on the hillside lay
  Whiter than snow;
Shepherds were watching them,
  Long, long ago.

Then from the happy sky,
  Angels bent low,
Singing their songs of joy,
  Long, long ago.

For in a manger bed,
  Cradled we know,
Christ came to Bethlehem
  Long, long ago.

Anonymous

Santa Claus

He comes in the night! He comes in the night!
  He softly, silently comes,
While the sweet little heads on the pillows so
    white
  Are dreaming of bugles and drums.
He cuts through the snow like a ship through
    the foam,
  While the white flakes 'round him whirl.
Who tells him I know not, but he finds the
    home
Of each good little boy and girl.

His sleigh is long, and deep, and wide.
  It will carry a host of things,
While dozens of drums hang over the side,
  With the sticks sticking under the strings.
And yet not the sound of a drum is heard,
  Not a bugle blast is blown,
As he mounts to the chimney-top like a bird,
  And drops to the hearth like a stone.

The little red stockings he silently fills,
  Till the stockings will hold no more.
The bright little sleds for the great snow hills
  Are quickly set down on the floor.
Then Santa Claus mounts to the roof like a
    bird,
  And glides to his seat in the sleigh.
Not the sound of a bugle or drum is heard
  As he noiselessly gallops away.

Anonymous, 1880

14

Secrets

Secrets big and secrets small
On the eve of Christmas.
Such keen ears has every wall
That we whisper, one and all,
On the eve of Christmas.

Secrets upstairs, secrets down,
On the eve of Christmas.
Daddy brings them from the town,
Wrapped in papers stiff and brown
On the eve of Christmas.

But the secret best of all,
On the eve of Christmas,
Steals right down the chimney tall,
Fills our stockings, one and all,
On the eve of Christmas.

Author Unknown

From:
Christmas Bells

I heard the bells
   on Christmas Day
Their old familiar
   carols play;
And wild and sweet
   the words repeat
Of peace on earth,
   good will to men.

Henry Wadsworth Longfellow

CHRISTMAS RECIPES

Christmas cooks young and old will produce the perfect sweet notes for a holiday celebration when they serve up the three delicious confections presented here. Use a cluster of the Christmas trees as a bright and jolly table centerpiece before slicing them up to serve as a Christmas treat along with the Viennese nut crescents and Danish sand cookies.

Christmas Trees

Ingredients:
(To make 8 trees 5″ tall)
¼ cup (½ stick) margarine
40 regular-sized
   marshmallows
½ cup toasted wheat germ

5 to 6 cups Rice Krispies
   or Puffed Rice
¼ cup tiny cinnamon hot
   candies or multi-colored
   sprinkles
Confectioners' sugar

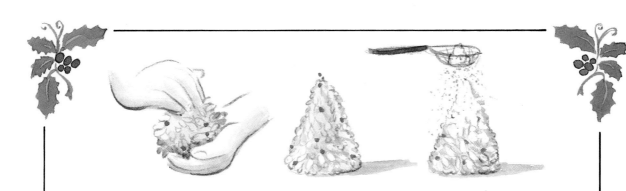

1. In double boiler, combine and melt margarine and marshmallows, stirring occasionally with wooden spoon over medium heat. Mixture will be completely melted in 10 to 15 minutes. Once melted, stir and cook about 2 minutes longer.

2. While marshmallows are melting, combine cereal, wheat germ, and most of the cinnamon hots or sprinkles in large mixing bowl.

3. When marshmallow mixture is ready, remove pan from stove. Use rubber scraper to scoop melted mixture into bowl.

Stir everything together well with wooden spoon. Stir until mixture develops spider-web-like threads between cereal bits.

4. Grease your hands with a little margarine. Break off a lump of cereal mixture and roll it into a ball about as wide as the palm of your hand. Then roll the top into a point to make a cone-shaped tree. Set tree on doily and top with one cinnamon hot pressed into tree tip. Sift a tiny bit of confectioners' sugar over tree top for "snow." Repeat to make more trees. Use cookie cutters to make other shapes.

Danish Sand Cookies

Ingredients:
(To make about 50
  cookies)
½ cup unsalted butter, at
  room temperature
1 cup granulated sugar
1 egg
1¾ cups all-purpose flour
¼ cup cornstarch
2 teaspoons baking
  powder
(To decorate cookies)
1 egg white, lightly beaten
1 cup almonds, blanched
  and halved or chopped
2 tablespoons granulated
  sugar
½ teaspoon cinnamon

1. Grease cookie sheets
and set aside. In large
bowl, beat together butter
and 1 cup sugar until light
and creamy. Add egg and
beat. Sift in flour,
cornstarch, and baking
powder and beat very
slowly until well mixed.

Set dough in refrigerator
to stiffen and chill for 30
minutes.
2. Break off about ⅓ of
dough and roll it out
between two sheets of
floured wax paper until
about ⅛" thick. Peel off
top paper, cut cookies
with cookie cutters, peel
away excess dough. Dip
spatula in flour, then use
it to lift cookies onto
greased baking sheet.
Repeat with remaining
dough. Preheat oven to
350°.
3. With pastry brush,
brush cookies with egg
white, then decorate with
nuts. In teacup, mix sugar
with cinnamon. Sprinkle
this over tops of cookies.
4. Bake cookies at 350°
for 8 to 10 minutes, or
until light gold around
edges. Cool cookies on
wire rack. Store airtight.

Viennese Nut Crescents

Ingredients:
(To make about 50
    cookies)
1 cup shelled unblanched
    hazelnuts (or blanched
    almonds, or walnuts)
1 cup unsalted butter
⅓ cup granulated sugar
2 egg yolks
1 teaspoon vanilla extract
2 cups all-purpose flour
1 teaspoon baking powder
Pinch of salt
¾ cup confectioners'
    sugar, sifted into bowl.

1. Finely chop nuts in
food processor or nut
chopper. Set aside.
Preheat oven to 350°.
Grease cookie sheets.
2. In large bowl, beat
together butter and
granulated sugar until
creamy. Add yolks and
vanilla and beat until
fluffy. Stir in flour, baking
powder, salt and chopped
nuts.
3. Pinch off small walnut-
size lumps of dough and
roll them on lightly
floured work surface.
Make rolls about as long
and thick as your middle
finger. Bend down ends
of rolls to form crescent
shape. Set rolls on greased
cookie sheets. Bake at
350° for 10 to 12 minutes,
or until pale golden. Cool
cookies on wire rack.
4. When cookies are still
slightly warm, gently roll
them in confectioners'
sugar, then return to wire
rack to cool. Store
airtight, with extra
confectioners' sugar sifted
on top.

THINGS TO MAKE FOR CHRISTMAS

Clay Christmas Tree Ornaments

What You Need:
A bowl
1/3 cup of water
1/2 cup of salt
1 cup of flour
Baking sheet
Rolling pin

Wax paper
Tin foil
Toothpick
Poster paint
Paint brushes
Shellac or varnish
Yarn

What to Do:
1. Make the clay by mixing the salt, water, and flour in a bowl.
2. Flatten dough and put it between two sheets of lightly floured wax paper. Roll out to about 1/4" thickness.
3. Cut out ornaments such as stars, animals, wreaths and tiny Christmas trees.
4. Place the ornaments on a baking sheet that is covered with foil.
5. With a toothpick, make a hole at the top of each ornament large enough to thread yarn through after the ornament is baked.

6. Set the oven at 275° F (135° C) and bake for one hour until brown. *Children should use the oven only with the help of parents.*
7. Let the ornaments cool and then paint them.
8. When the paint is dry, coat the ornaments with shellac or varnish.
9. String the shapes with yarn and hang them on your Christmas tree.

Christmas Tree Chains

This Christmas, give your tree a traditional feeling by making chains and pomander balls to hang from its branches. Both decorations provide a homey touch, and the sweet and spicy smell of the pomander ball will delight you.

To make chains, use a darning needle and thread to string popcorn, cranberries, and any other decorative materials you like (see illustrations below). When the chain is the size you prefer, tie a knot in the thread. The chain is then ready to hang on your tree!

Popcorn

Cranberry and Popcorn

Drinking Straws and Paper Cutouts

Dry Macaroni

Old–Fashioned Pomander Ball

What You'll Need

Lemon
Cinnamon
Ginger

Box of cloves
Ribbon or yarn
Paper bag

What to Do

Stick cloves into the lemon so that all of its surface is covered. Put the lemon into a paper bag. Pour a little ginger and cinnamon into the bag. Close the bag and shake it so that spices cover the lemon. Tie ribbon or yarn around the lemon so that you can hang it on your tree.

Pomander balls last for a long time. After a period of time, however, they will no longer smell spicy.

THE TWELVE DAYS OF CHRISTMAS

*On the first day of Christmas
my true love sent to me,
a partridge in a pear tree.*

On the second day of Christmas
my true love sent to me,
two turtle doves,
and a partridge in a pear tree.

On the third day of Christmas
my true love sent to me,
three French hens,
two turtle doves,
and a partridge in a pear tree.

On the fourth day of Christmas
my true love sent to me,
four calling birds, three French hens,
two turtle doves,
and a partridge in a pear tree.

On the fifth day of Christmas
my true love sent to me,
five gold rings,
four calling birds, three French hens,
two turtle doves,
and a partridge in a pear tree.

On the sixth day of Christmas
my true love sent to me,
six geese a-laying, five gold rings,
four calling birds, three French hens,
two turtle doves,
and a partridge in a pear tree.

On the seventh day of Christmas
my true love sent to me,
seven swans a-swimming,
six geese a-laying, five gold rings,
four calling birds, three French hens,
two turtle doves,
and a partridge in a pear tree.

On the eighth day of Christmas
my true love sent to me,
eight maids a-milking,
seven swans a-swimming,
six geese a-laying, five gold rings,
four calling birds, three French hens,
two turtle doves,
and a partridge in a pear tree.

On the ninth day of Christmas
my true love sent to me,
nine ladies dancing, eight maids a-milking,
seven swans a-swimming,
six geese a-laying, five gold rings,
four calling birds, three French hens,
two turtle doves,
and a partridge in a pear tree.

On the tenth day of Christmas
my true love sent to me,
ten lords a-leaping,
nine ladies dancing, eight maids a-milking,
seven swans a-swimming,
six geese a-laying, five gold rings,
four calling birds, three French hens,
two turtle doves,
and a partridge in a pear tree.

On the eleventh day of Christmas
my true love sent to me,
eleven pipers piping, ten lords a-leaping,
nine ladies dancing, eight maids a-milking,
seven swans a-swimming,
six geese a-laying, five gold rings,
four calling birds, three French hens,
two turtle doves,
and a partridge in a pear tree.

On the twelfth day of Christmas
my true love sent to me,
twelve drummers drumming,
eleven pipers piping, ten lords a-leaping,
nine ladies dancing, eight maids a-milking,
seven swans a-swimming,
six geese a-laying, five gold rings,
four calling birds, three French hens,
two turtle doves,
and a partridge in a pear tree.

CHRISTMAS IN OTHER LANDS

Christmas is celebrated in almost every country in the world. The true meaning of the holiday remains the same everywhere, but every country has its own special—and charming—Christmas customs.

Sweden

In Sweden, the Christmas celebration begins on St. Lucia's Day, December 13. Lucia was a young Sicilian girl who lived in the fourth century and believed in Christ. When she refused to marry a man who did not share her belief, she was executed, and 200 years later she was made a saint.

Early in the morning on St. Lucia's Day, the eldest daughter in a Swedish family plays St. Lucia. Wearing a white robe and a crown of lighted candles, she brings everyone else in the house coffee and cakes. Each town in Sweden also elects a St. Lucia who leads a parade of young people in a day-long celebration.

Christmas Eve is a merry occasion in Sweden. The celebration begins in the afternoon with a meal that lasts for hours. Then the candles on the Christmas tree are lit.

Sweden's version of Santa Claus is Jultomten, a tiny gnome. On Christmas Eve, when everyone is sleeping, he arrives in a sleigh pulled by a goat and leaves his presents.

Italy

Christmas is a time of feasting in Italy. A traditional custom is to bake Magi Cakes and present them to friends. The bigger the cake, the greater the esteem it shows. It is said that many years ago an Italian nobleman received a Magi Cake measuring more than twenty feet across, decorated with his coat of arms.

The Christmas season lasts for three weeks in Italy, from the Novena eight days before Christmas until the Twelfth Night, or Epiphany, January 6. Many Italians fast for twenty-four hours before Christmas. On Christmas Eve, they eat an elaborate meal at which pasta, fish, and pastries are traditionally served.

Italians give gifts on Epiphany, not on Christmas. The Santa Claus of Italy is not a man but a woman called La Befana. (*Befana* is the Italian word for Epiphany.) La Befana brings gifts on Epiphany Eve, when the Magi, the wise men from the East, were journeying to Bethlehem to pay homage to the infant Jesus. Legend has it that the Magi asked La Befana to lead them to Bethlehem, but she said she couldn't because she had to clean her house.

Afterwards, she was sorry, and that is why she now travels the world, searching for the Christ child. In Italy, she goes from house to house, leaving children presents in their shoes. Like Santa Claus, she comes down the chimney, but she arrives on a broomstick instead of a sleigh. She only leaves presents for good children. Bad children receive a piece of coal or a birch rod.

The traditional Italian version of a Christmas tree is a *ceppo,* a kind of lattice-work pyramid whose shelves are elaborately decorated with colored paper and many tiny objects. Underneath the ceppo, the Italians place the creche or *precepio.* The precepio is left empty until Christmas Day, when a baby, the Christ child, is placed in it.

SONGS OF CHRISTMAS

The First Noel

TRADITIONAL

16TH CENTURY, FRENCH

The__ first__ No - el the__ an - gels did say Was to cer - tain poor shep-herds in fields as they lay. In__ fields__ where__ they lay__ keep-ing their sheep On a cold win - ter's night__ that

was__ so deep. No - el,__ No - el, No - el, No -

el,__ Born is the King__ of Is - ra - el.

2. They looked up and saw a star
   Shining in the east beyond them far,
   And to the earth it gave great light.
   And so it continued both day and night.
   CHORUS

3. And by the light of that same star,
   Three wise men came from country far,
   To seek for a King was their intent.
   And to follow the star wherever it went.
   CHORUS

4. This star drew nigh to the northwest,
   O'er Bethlehem it took its rest,
   And there it did both stop and stay
   Right o'er the place where Jesus lay.
   CHORUS

5. Then enter'd in those wise men three,
   Full reverently upon their knee,
   And offer'd there in His presence,
   Their gold and myrrh and frankincense.
   CHORUS

6. Then let us all with one accord
   Sing praises to our heav'nly Lord,
   That hath made heav'n and earth of nought,
   And with His blood mankind hath bought.
   CHORUS

Jingle Bells

J. S. PIERPONT, 1857

Dash-ing thro' the snow, In a one-horse o-pen sleigh,

O'er the fields we go, Laugh-ing all the way.____

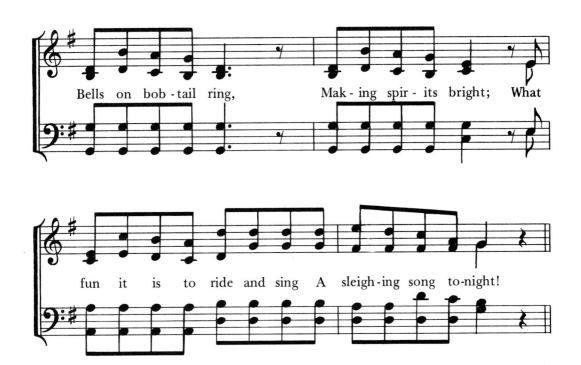

Bells on bob-tail ring, Mak-ing spir-its bright; What

fun it is to ride and sing A sleigh-ing song to-night!

Jin - gle bells, jin - gle bells, jin - gle all the way;

Oh, what fun it is to ride in a one-horse o -pen sleigh.—

Jin - gle bells, jin - gle bells, jin - gle all the way;

Oh, what fun it is to ride in a one-horse o - pen sleigh!

CHRISTMAS IN THE 19th CENTURY

A Christmas Dinner

A Reminiscence by
Charles Dickens

Who can be insensible to the outpourings of good feeling, and the honest interchange of affectionate attachment which abound at this season of the year? A Christmas family-party! We know nothing in nature more delightful!

The Christmas family-party that we mean, is not a mere assemblage of relations, got up at a week or two's notice, originating this year, having no family precedent in the last, and not likely to be repeated in the next. No. It is an annual gathering of all the accessible members of the family, young or old, rich or poor; and all the children look forward to it, for two months beforehand, in a fever of anticipation. Formerly it was held at grandpapa's; but grandpapa getting old, and grandmamma getting old too, and rather infirm, they have given up housekeeping, and domesticated themselves with uncle George; so, the party always takes place at uncle George's house, but grandmamma sends in most of the good things, and grandpapa always will toddle down, all the way to Newgate market, to buy the turkey, which he

engages a porter to bring home behind him in triumph, always insisting on the man's being rewarded with a glass of spirits, over and above his hire, to drink "a merry Christmas and a happy new year" to aunt George.

On Christmas Eve, grandmamma is always in excellent spirits, and after employing all the children during the day, in stoning the plums, and all that, insists, regularly every year, on uncle

George coming down into the kitchen, taking off his coat, and stirring the pudding for half an hour or so, which uncle George good-humoredly does to the vociferous delight of the children and servants. The evening concludes with a glorious game of blind-man's bluff, in an early stage of which grandpapa takes great care to be caught, in order that he may have an opportunity of displaying his dexterity.

On the following morning, the old couple, with as many of the children

as the pew will hold, go to church in great state, leaving aunt George at home dusting decanters and filling castors, and uncle George carrying bottles into the dining-parlor, and calling for corkscrews, and getting into everybody's way.

When the church-party returns to lunch, grandpapa produces a small sprig of mistletoe from his pocket, and tempts the boys to kiss their little cousins under it—a proceeding which affords both the boys and the old gentleman unlimited satisfaction, but which rather outrages grandmamma's ideas of decorum, until grandpapa says, that when he was just thirteen years and three months old he kissed grandmamma under a mistletoe too, on which the children clap their hands, and laugh very heartily, as do aunt George and uncle George; and grandmamma looks pleased, and says, with a benevolent smile, that grandpapa was an impudent young dog, on which the children laugh very heartily again, and grandpapa more heartily than any of them.

Suddenly a hackney-coach is heard to stop, and uncle George, who has been looking out of the window, exclaims, "Here's Jane!" and uncle Robert and aunt Jane, and the dear little baby, and the nurse, and the whole party, are ushered upstairs amidst tumultuous shouts of "Oh, my!" from the children, and frequently repeated warnings not to hurt baby from the nurse. And grandpapa takes the child, and grandmamma kisses her daughter, and the confusion of this first entry has scarcely subsided, when some other aunts and uncles with more cousins arrive . . . and nothing is to be heard but a confused din of talking, laughing, and merriment.

As to the dinner, it's perfectly delightful . . . uncle George tells stories, and carves poultry, and takes wine, and jokes with the children . . . and exhilarates everybody with his good humor and hospitality; and when, at last, a stout servant staggers in with a gigantic pudding, with a sprig of holly on the top, there is such a laughing, and shouting, and clapping of little chubby hands, and kicking up of fat dumpy legs, as can only be equalled by the applause with which the astonishing feat of pouring lighted brandy into mince-pies, is received by the younger visitors. Then the dessert!   and the wine!   and the fun! Such beautiful speeches, and *such* songs. Even grandpapa not only sings his annual song with unprecedented vigor, but on being honored with an unanimous *encore,* according to annual custom, actually comes out with a new one which nobody but grandmamma ever heard before.

And thus the evening passes, in a strain of rational good-will and cheerfulness, doing more to awaken the sympathies of every member of the party in behalf of his neighbor, and to perpetuate their good feeling, during the ensuing year, than half the homilies that have ever been written, by half the Divines that have ever lived.

*(from **Sketches by Boz**)*

THE GOLD COINS

A Story by
The Brothers Grimm

Once upon a time, there was a little girl whose father and mother had died. She was so poor that she did not have a room to live in or a bed to sleep in. She had nothing she could call her own but the clothes she wore and a small piece of bread that a kind person had given her.

Still, she was a good, pious child, and when it seemed that all the world had forsaken her, she kept her trust in God. One day, she went out into the countryside and there she met a poor man who said, "Please give me something to eat. I am so hungry." The kind girl handed him her piece of bread and said, "May God bless it to your use."

She walked on and met a child who moaned and said, "My head is so cold, please give me something to cover it with." So she took off her cap and gave it to the child. When she had walked a little farther, she met another child who had no coat and was frozen with cold, and she gave the child her coat. In a little while, she met another child who asked her for her blouse, and she gave that away, too.

At last she came to a forest. By then it was dark, and yet another child came along. This child asked her for her shift and the good-hearted girl thought: "It's

dark now and no one will see me. I can give my shift away." So she took it off and gave it to the child.

Then, as she stood there with nothing left to give away, stars began to fall from the heavens, and the stars turned out to be bright gold coins. Even though

she had given her shift away, she now had on a new one made of the very finest linen.

Then she collected the coins in her skirt, and she was rich for the rest of her life.

CHRISTMAS GREENERY

The Christmas holiday would be far less festive without Christmas trees, holly, and mistletoe to brighten up the scene—and each of these Christmas decorations has a fascinating history behind its use.

Mistletoe

In Great Britain more than 2,000 years ago, the pagan Druids thought mistletoe was a sacred plant. Today kissing under the mistletoe is supposed to bring good luck. This custom began in Scandinavia.

Holly

According to legend, the crown of thorns that Christ wore was made of holly. His blood flowing over the holly berries turned them from white to red.

Christmas Trees

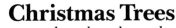

Evergreens have long been thought of as symbolizing life because they keep their leaves all through the year. Pagan peoples brought evergreen branches indoors to celebrate a festival. The custom of putting up and decorating trees may have started in Germany when Martin Luther saw the stars shining above a pine tree on Christmas Eve, and put up a tree of his own, decorated with candles.

OUR CHRISTMAS TREE

We know that Christmas is really here when our tree goes up and that delicious evergreen aroma fills the house.

Describe the high points of trimming your tree below and paste in a photograph of the tree.

When we put up our tree _____

Who helped trim it _____

_____

Who put on the highest ornament _____

OUR CHRISTMAS EVE

Making sure the tree looks *perfect* . . . lighting the Yule log . . .
wrapping last-minute presents . . . hanging the Christmas stockings . . .
leaving a light on so Santa doesn't stumble in the dark . . . is there
anything to match the expectant excitement of the last hours of
Christmas Eve? *Describe your Christmas Eve below.*

*Who was here*_____

_____

_____

*What we had to eat*_____

_____

*What we did on Christmas Eve*_____

_____

_____

_____

OUR CHRISTMAS DAY

The presents have been opened . . . the Christmas visitors begin to arrive . . . the delicious smells of Christmas dinner fill the house . . . it's Christmas Day! Merry Christmas to one and all! *Describe your Christmas Day below.*

When we opened our presents _____

_____

_____

Who came to visit _____

_____

_____

What we had for Christmas dinner _____

_____

_____

_____

_____

What else we did on Christmas day _____

_____

_____

_____

_____

_____

_____

OUR
FAVORITE GIFTS

The true meaning of Christmas is based on the idea of love and giving. The best presents are not the biggest or most expensive ones but those which perfectly express this idea. *List your favorite gifts below, describing what they were, who gave them, and who received them.*

_____

_____

_____

_____

_____

_____

_____

_____

_____

_____

_____

OUR CHRISTMAS PHOTO ALBUM

Christmas is the happiest time, and one of the season's most rewarding pleasures is to snap pictures of your family as they enjoy this year's festive celebration.

Paste your favorite Christmas photos on these pages.

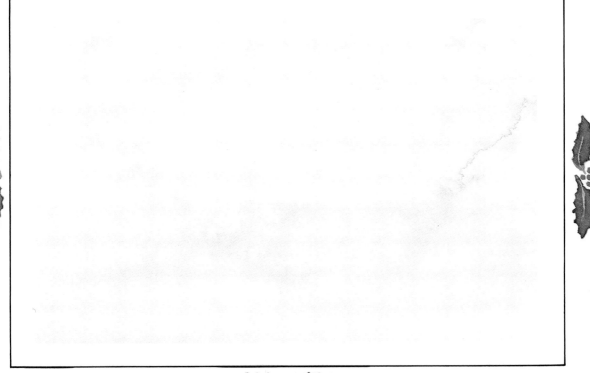

OUR SPECIAL
CHRISTMAS CARDS

Paste the cards
you liked best this Christmas
(including your own!)
on these pages.

A Christmas Wish

God bless the master of this house,
 Likewise the mistress, too.
May their barns be filled with wheat and corn
 And their hearts be always true.

A merry Christmas is our wish
 Wherever we do appear.
To you a well-filled purse, a well-filled dish
 And a happy, bright new year!

Traditional English Carol

A CHRISTMAS JOURNEY

by Hans Wilhelm

A long time ago,
two mice named Judith and Jed
lived in a small land
ruled by soldiers
from across the sea.

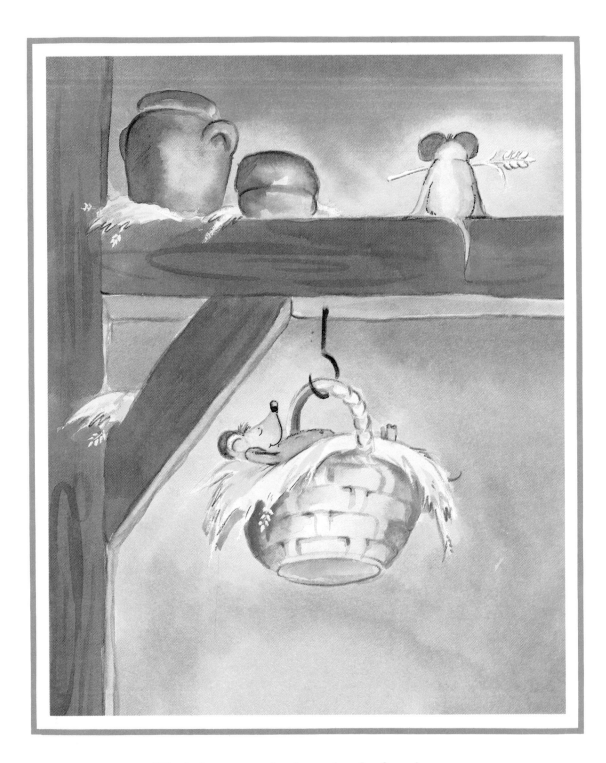

Their home was in the attic of a farmhouse
at the edge of a field.

It was a nice, cozy place, and best of all, it kept them safe from
their enemy, Brutus the cat.

Winter came and snow covered the
ground. It snowed for days and finally
the mice ate all of the food they had
stored away. Every day, they sneaked
out to the barn to look for more food.
But they didn't find any.

The snow kept falling and the mice
became hungrier. One day, Jed said,
"We must find something to eat or we'll
starve."

"But there isn't a morsel to be had,"
Judith said. "Even Brutus is hungry."

"Then we'll have to leave here and
find food somewhere else," said Jed.

Judith sighed. "It's so nice and cozy here," she said.
"But you're right. We'll go tonight when Brutus is asleep."

After it became dark, Jed and Judith tiptoed out of the farmhouse. The night was still. The sky was black. Snow covered the fields. The mice were very cold as they trudged along.

"I hope we don't meet a robber," Judith said.

"SShh!" said Jed. "I just heard a noise. I think someone is following us."

Quickly they ducked under a rock. Hidden from sight, they huddled together in the darkness, shivering with cold and fright.

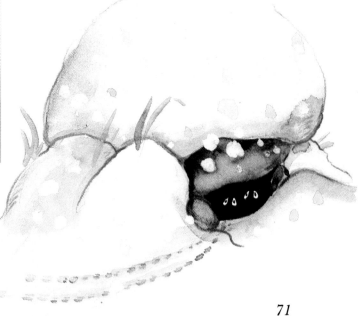

In the morning, Judith sniffed the air.

"I smell smoke," she said.

"Let's see where it's coming from," Jed said. "Someone may be cooking something."

Three men were asleep around a small fire. A donkey stood tied to a tree. A ring of boxes and trunks circled the men.

"If only there's some food," Judith said.

"Yes, if only," Jed agreed. "I've never been this hungry before."

Careful not to make a sound, they looked in all the boxes and trunks. But there was no food.

Instead, there were great piles of coins and jewels and gold objects.
"We could take some of the coins," Jed said. "Then we could buy some food."
"That would be stealing," Judith said.

"But these men are probably robbers," said Jed. "They must have stolen all of this stuff."
"It still wouldn't be right to take something that isn't ours," Judith replied.

Suddenly, out of the corner of his eye,
Jed saw a dark shadow moving across
the snow. "It's Brutus," he whispered.
"Quick, let's get into this trunk."

The two mice were still hungry, but it was dark and
warm inside the trunk and they soon fell asleep. When
they woke up, the trunk was bouncing up and down like
a ship in a storm.

They lifted the lid slowly and peeped out. It was night
again. The three men were walking along, and the boxes
and trunks were piled high on the donkey's back.

"At least this is better than walking," Jed said.

"Yes, but we don't know where we are going," Judith
replied as she closed her eyes again.

After a while, the donkey stopped. Jed and Judith lifted the lid again. They were in a small village. The streets were crowded with soldiers and people. The three men were talking to a fourth man.

"I think it's time to get out of here," Jed said. They scrambled out of the trunk and off the donkey's back.

"I see a bakery," said Judith. "Let's take a look inside."

The bakery was empty. The shelves and
barrels were bare. "I don't understand this,"
Judith said.

"Let's try the grocer's," said Jed.

There was no food in the grocer's either, and
no food in all the other stores they tried. There
was no food anywhere.

"Something funny is going on here," said Jed. "These people have eaten every scrap of food in the village. But why are they all here?"

Suddenly, they heard a familiar growl. "It's Brutus!" Jed said.

"Let's get into the center of the crowd over there," Judith said. "He won't see us then."

They moved along with the crowd, and when everyone stopped, Jed and Judith scampered to the front of the group. They were in a small room that was filled with people.

The mice gasped. Before them was a huge pile of things: boxes and trunks full of gold, bags of jewels with bright stones spilling out, rolls of silk and velvet cloth, and . . . FOOD! . . . baskets and jars and dishes piled high with cakes and fruits and cheese and loaves of bread.

But none of the people was paying any attention to the treasures on the floor. They were looking instead at a cradle around which the presents were arranged. In the cradle was a tiny infant.

"Food at last," Jed cried, ready to start nibbling.
Judith pulled him back. "No, you can't," she said.
"All of these things are gifts for the child.
We can't touch them."
She thought for a moment.
"We should give him a gift, too, Jed."
She took off her scarf and placed it
alongside the other gifts.
The child's face glowed
and he seemed to smile.
It was as if he were saying,
"Let us all enjoy this together."
So they did.
And Jed and Judith knew that, at last,
they had found a new home.

HAPPY
NEW YEAR

Peace. Joy. Health.
And the Spirit of Christmas All through the Year.

Your New Year's Wish

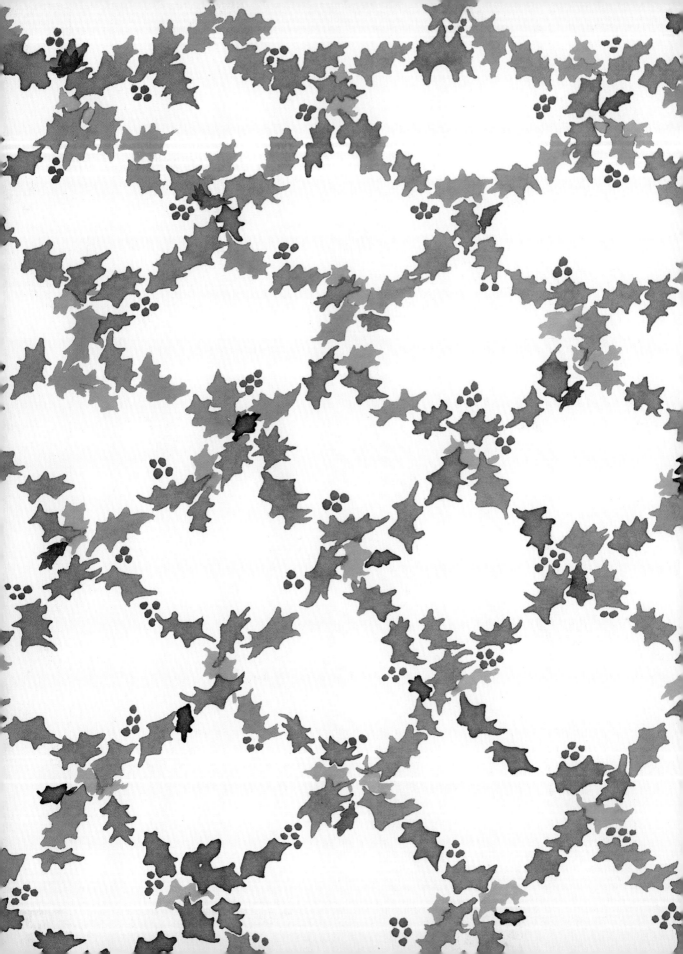